HOW SCIENCE WORKS

TRUCKS, TRACTORS, AND CRANES

BRYSON GORE

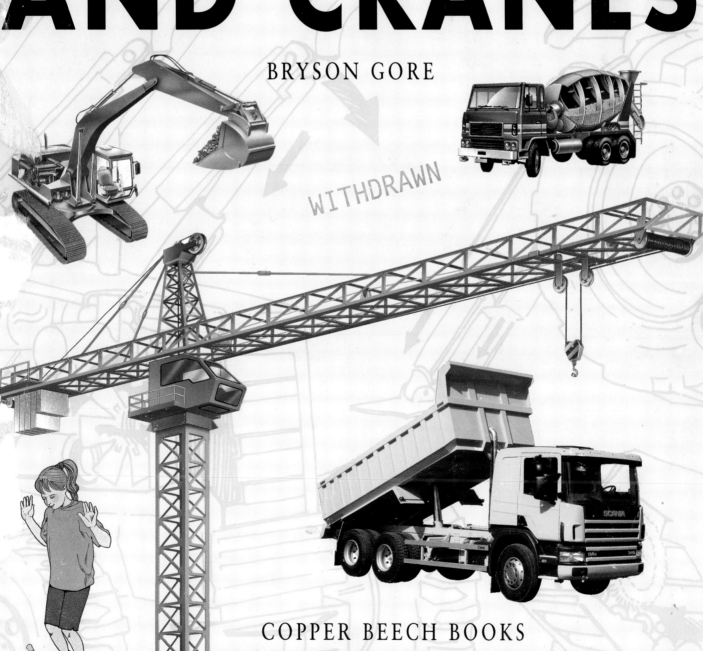

COPPER BEECH BOOKS
BROOKFIELD • CONNECTICUT

CONTENTS

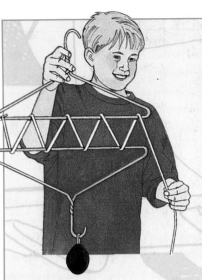

THE SCIENCE OF MACHINES

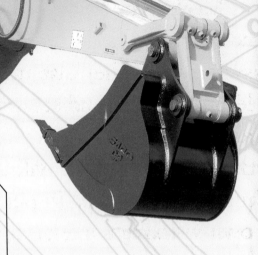

INTRODUCTION

Trucks, tractors, and cranes lift and move heavy loads. They are some of the most important machines that we use today.

Modern tractors and cranes use complex hydraulic and electronic systems. But they also use the science of levers, pulleys, and screws that have been around for 4,000 years. As you discover how these simple machines work you will understand how complex modern machines operate. To put these ideas into action, build your own working crane or digger as you read the book.

To make the projects, you will need: thick and thin cardboard, single-sided corrugated cardboard, a craft knife, 3 or 4 pebbles, scissors, PVA glue, acrylic paint, 1/4 in diameter wooden dowel, screw eyelets and hook, string, a thin rubber band about 1/2 in long, 2 headless matchsticks, a large wooden bead, and 4 empty thread spools.

Model crane project box

Science experiment project box

© Aladdin Books Ltd 2000

Designed and produced by
Aladdin Books Ltd
28 Percy Street
London W1P 0LD

First published in
the United States in 2000 by
Copper Beech Books,
an imprint of
The Millbrook Press
2 Old New Milford Road
Brookfield, Connecticut 06804

ISBN 0-7613-1209-9 (lib. bdg.)
0-7613-0836-9 (pbk.)

Cataloging-in-Publication data is
on file at the Library of Congress

Printed in Belgium
Editor
Jim Pipe

Series Design
David West Children's Books

Designer
Simon Morse

Illustrators
Ian Thompson, Catherine Ward,
Simon Tegg, Alex Pang, Gerald
Witcomb, Don Simpson, Aziz
Khan, David Russell, Ron
Hayward, Graham White,
Peter Harper, Ross Watton,
and Simon Bishop.

Picture Research
Brooks Krikler Research

THE SCIENCE OF MACHINES

The strongest human body can only push or pull an object so much in order to move it around or lift it up against the force of gravity. Machines allow us to push or pull with a bigger force.

The first machines changed the forces from our own bodies. Modern machines use forces in the same way but are powered by an engine.

Early machines were powered by humans or animals. The invention of the steam engine allowed machines to produce their own power for the first time.

STABILITY

All machines are designed to be stable—they are made so they don't tip over. But this can happen very easily if they are lifting very heavy loads or moving over bumpy ground. On pages 8 and 9 we look at how trucks and cranes are built to stay upright.

BACKHOE LOADER

A powerful engine creates power for lifting and moving.

DIESEL POWER

Modern machines need to provide power. All modern machines have engines to supply the energy needed, and they usually get their power by burning a fuel such as diesel. Turn to page 18 to find out more.

Liquid pumped along pipes powers the attachments on machines like this backhoe loader. This way of changing forces is called hydraulics. Find out how hydraulics work on page 20.

CRANES

Cranes are machines that lift loads into the air. Some cranes are mobile, but the biggest ones are attached to the ground. Learn how both types use levers and pulleys on page 14.

Mobile crane

The cab provides a safe place for the operator to control the machine.

Different attachments mean that one vehicle can apply forces in different ways to suit any job. Turn to page 26 to find out more.

Chunky tires spread out the force of gravity and give a good grip in muddy conditions.

actor

BIG WHEELS

Any heavy machine pushes down on the ground. But a machine that works on soft or muddy ground needs to spread the force of gravity over the biggest possible area. Find out how on page 6.

CHAPTER 1 – TRACKS

All mobile machines need to push and pull against the ground to move around. Some use tracks instead of wheels because on uneven ground the wheels might lift off, making the machine unstable. Tracks spread the weight out evenly, and part of the track is always in contact with the ground.

This heavy machine uses tracks to remain stable while working on uneven ground.

Try this—do studs give a better grip?

No studs   Studs

Traction

Traction is the scientific word for grip. Playing sports on a muddy field would be dangerous without good grip. The studs on a soccer cleat help you start, stop, and turn without slipping.

The tracks on this bulldozer grip like the studs on a cleat.

CAT F 973

CAT

SNOW PLOW

Snow plows often combine wheels for steering and tracks for grip. Snow can fill the tread on wheels but falls off the tracks as they turn.

TRACKS

Tracks are made from many individual links joined together to form a flexible band around two wheels at the front and back of the vehicle. When the wheels turn, the whole track turns and pushes against the ground, giving more grip.

To keep themselves from sinking in soft ground, some machines have lots of wheels and a big tread (*right*). Tread is the spacing of the grooves and ridges on a tire. Each wheel has its own system of springs so that all wheels stay in contact with the ground.

MODEL CRANE
PART 1

WHEEL BASE

1 MAKE THE BASE
To make your model crane, first trace section **A** onto thick cardboard from the plan at the end of the book. Cut **A** out and fold it along the dotted lines. Then glue the end and side flaps together. When the glue is dry, paint your wheel base.

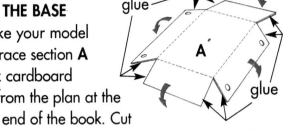

2 ADD THE WHEELS
Collect 4 empty thread spools. You will need 2 pieces of wooden dowel or 2 pencils 8 in long. Fit each dowel into a thread spool then push the dowel through the axle holes. Then attach another spool to the other end.

3 MAKE THE TRACKS
Cut out the tracks from single-sided corrugated cardboard, and glue **C** and **D** to the smooth side of **B**.

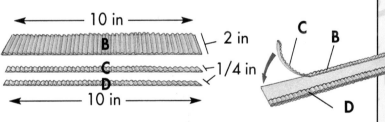

4 ATTACH THE TRACKS
Now paint the tracks. When they are dry, wrap them around the wheels and glue the ends together.

STABILITY

Machines need to be both balanced and stable. Balanced means that they do not fall over on their own. Stable means that if they do lean over they fall back to their original position.

An object is balanced if the center of gravity (the average position of the weight) is between the wheels. It is stable until the center of gravity moves outside the wheels. Keeping the weight near to the ground makes things more stable.

Adding weight to the base of your model will make it more stable.

A dump truck is well balanced when the dumper is down. As it lifts up, its load moves toward the back. If the truck is stable, its front wheels will not lift off the ground.

Weight of load

ON A SLOPE

Tractors and diggers often have to drive across sloping ground. Early tractors tipped over if the slope was too great. Modern tractors are built with the weight kept low to make them more stable.

STABLE CRANES

Cranes need to be able to hold heavy loads (A) away from their base. To keep them from falling over, a counterweight (B) is held on the opposite side to ensure that the center of gravity remains over the base.

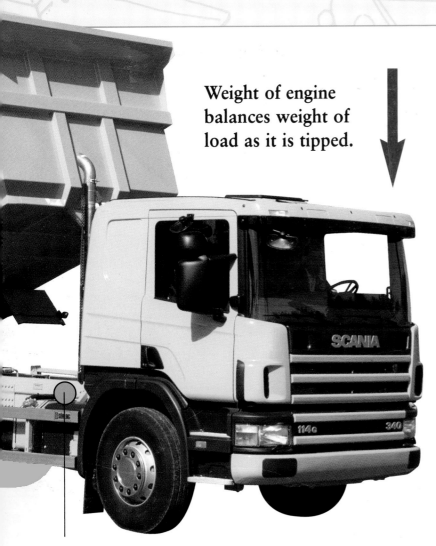

Weight of engine balances weight of load as it is tipped.

If center of gravity is between wheels truck stays stable.

Stability project

1 Fix a coin in one end of a matchbox so that it sticks out to the side. If the coin is at the top, the box will fall over easily if you push it to the side.

2 Now put the coin at the bottom. You can tip the box over a long way and it stands up again when you let go.

3 How far does the coin need to be sticking out at the top for the box to fall without pushing.

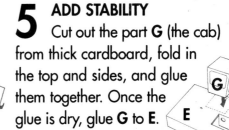

MODEL CRANE
PART 2
THE BODY

1 MAKE THE BODY
Trace part **E** from the plans and cut from thick cardboard. Then fold in the sides and glue them together. Don't forget to cut out holes **E1, E2, E3, E4,** and **E5**!

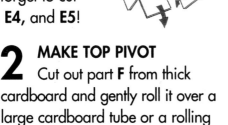

2 MAKE TOP PIVOT
Cut out part **F** from thick cardboard and gently roll it over a large cardboard tube or a rolling pin. Then glue its ends together.

3 ATTACH TOP PIVOT
Glue part **F** to the underside of part **E** making sure that hole **E5** lines up with the center of **F**.

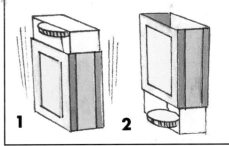

4 MAKE IT STABLE
Glue 3 or 4 medium-sized pebbles inside the back of base **E**. These make it more stable.

5 ADD STABILITY
Cut out the part **G** (the cab) from thick cardboard, fold in the top and sides, and glue them together. Once the glue is dry, glue **G** to **E**.

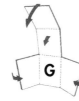

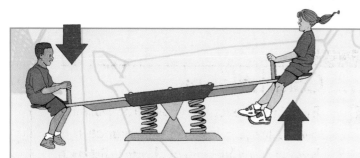

A seesaw is an example of a 1st-class lever. A smaller person sitting further away from the fulcrum can balance a heavier person nearer the fulcrum.

CHAPTER 2 – LEVERS AND PULLEYS

Levers and pulleys are two of the simplest parts of any machine and can be thought of as simple machines in their own right. They allow us to change the size and direction of forces to match a load. Although the size of the force can be changed, the total energy supplied always remains the same.

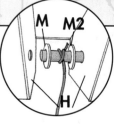

A crowbar is also a simple lever. By moving our lever (the crowbar) a long way, we can move a heavy object (the rock) a short distance.

MODEL CRANE
PART 3
THE CRANE ARM

1 MAKE THE CRANE ARM
Cut out two part Hs from thick cardboard and cut out a hole in each. Then glue them to **E**. But make sure holes **E3** and **E2** line up with the holes in the two part **H**s.

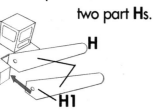

2 ADD SUPPORTS
Cut out parts **J** and **I** from thick cardboard and glue them to the arm. Get an adult to help you cut a 3 in length of dowel (or pencil) and screw an eyelet half way along the dowel. Glue this to the arm with the eyelet pointing downward.

3 MAKE HOOK
Screw an eyelet and a hook into opposite sides of a wooden bead.

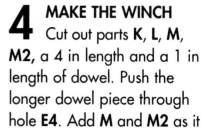

4 MAKE THE WINCH
Cut out parts **K, L, M, M2**, a 4 in length and a 1 in length of dowel. Push the longer dowel piece through hole **E4**. Add **M** and **M2** as it goes through. Glue the 1 in dowel to **K**. Then glue **K** to the longer dowel and **L** to the other end.

4 in dowel

L

K

1 in

Coin balance

By using a lever, a small force pushing over a large distance can balance a bigger force moving a shorter distance. Make a simple balance with a ruler and a sharp edge. Try to balance a coin using a similar-sized coin (**1**) and then with one half its weight (**2**). How much further do you have to place the smaller coin from the fulcrum?

1   **2**

This crane (*left*) uses a pulley (top) to lift its load and a lever (bottom) to move the pulley to the correct position.

HOW LEVERS WORK

Levers are used with forces that turn around the fulcrum, a point where the lever pivots or turns. If we use a longer lever the force applied to the load increases, but we need to move the lever a greater distance to lift the load by the same amount.

HOW PULLEYS WORK

A simple pulley allows us to change the direction of the force that we apply (the effort). This allows the person or machine doing the pulling to remain on the ground. Compound pulleys increase the size of the force allowing us to lift much heavier loads.

Effort

COMPOUND PULLEY

Effort

SIMPLE PULLEY

Load   Load

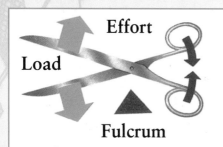

Effort

Load

Fulcrum

A pair of scissors combines two second-class levers. Depending upon where the object to be cut is held, the force is increased or reduced.

COMBINING LEVERS

In machines such as excavators, several levers are often used together. This is called a compound lever. Because the levers do not bend, they swivel at a number of different points. They allow a digger to apply the force where it is needed and to make the force bigger or smaller to match the job.

CLASSES OF LEVERS

There are three classes or types of lever depending upon which side of the fulcrum the effort and load are.

1ST CLASS

Load

Fulcrum

Effort

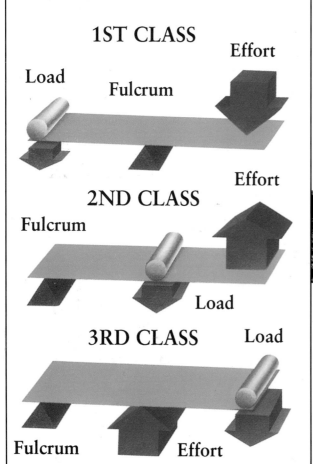

2ND CLASS

Fulcrum

Effort

Load

3RD CLASS

Load

Fulcrum   Effort

BOOM

Fulcrum

Load

Effort

A wheelbarrow is an example of a second-class lever. The load is close to the fulcrum so the effort needs to travel a long way to lift the load a short distance.

Load   Fulcrum

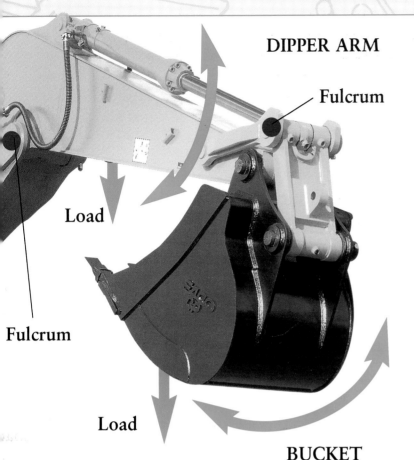

DIPPER ARM

Fulcrum

Load

Fulcrum

Load

BUCKET

The depth of a hole the excavator can dig depends on the length of its dipper arm and boom. This excavator can dig a hole 20 feet deep.

EXCAVATOR

An excavator is a complex machine that combines three levers— the boom, the dipper arm, and the bucket.

The boom is a third-class lever that raises or lowers the dipper. The dipper is a first-class lever that moves the bucket in and out. The bucket is itself another first-class lever that tilts to dig a hole and empty its load.

RAMPS

A ramp is another example of a simple machine. A wedge is another name for a ramp.

We use ramps to help us increase the distance over which we move an object in order to lift it against gravity.

The ancient Egyptians used ramps to help lift stones for the pyramids, and you can see ramps on any modern building site.

Ramp

LIVING LEVERS

The skeletons of living creatures contain many levers. The human forearm is one of the few examples of a third-class lever. Here, the large force of the muscle travels a short distance to make the hand move an object over a large distance.

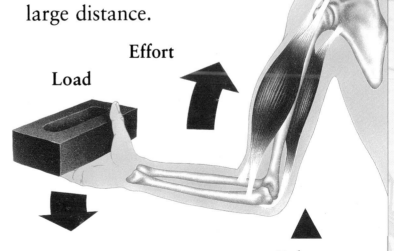

Effort

Load

Fulcrum

DOCKSIDE CRANES

Large cranes, either fixed or on railroad lines, are used to move cargo from ships to trains and trucks for delivery inland.

This crane (*right*) shows the incredible loads that can be carried by compound pulleys.

The control cab for a tower crane is at the top.

The operator has a clear view of the load and building site and can move the arm to where it is needed.

CRANES

Cranes are the most common big machines that use pulleys. Because pulleys use cable, they can only pull things upward (unlike levers which can push *and* pull).

Cranes need to be rigid (stiff) structures that will support the pulley system above the load.

Test out your own pulley system.

Control cab

Concrete counterweights

Pulling power

Make a compound pulley using two coat hangers. Tie the string to the top hanger and then loop it around the bottom hanger. Every loop will increase the mechanical advantage—that is, you can pull a heavier weight by pulling the string further.

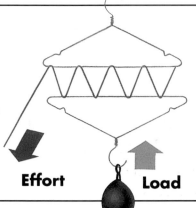

Effort   Load

TOWER CRANE

Tower cranes are used in the construction of modern skyscrapers. At first the crane does not need to be very tall, but as the building grows so must the crane (see *below*). Normally, the crane stands inside what will become the elevator shaft of the finished building—and the only problem is how to remove the crane once the last story of the building is complete.

Jib

The jib, or main arm, of a tower crane is made from steel struts.

The counterweight is used to balance the weight of the jib, which is greater than any load it would need to lift.

Mobile crane

The load is lifted by a compound pulley system mounted on a trolley. This can be changed for light or heavy loads.

The trolley moves in and out along the jib, and the jib turns to position the load.

Load

MOBILE CRANES

Mobile cranes can be used in more places than tower cranes but need special legs to make sure they are stable. The main arm of the crane is often built from a series of levers so that the load can be positioned more accurately.

Tower cranes can build themselves by raising the cab and jib on hydraulic rams and then lifting the next section of tower into place (*right*). Some cranes are over 600 ft tall.

Tower crane

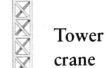

SCREWS

Any screw is a simple machine in its own right, like the pulley and lever. It is used to change a turning force into a force that goes in a straight line.

We often use the thread to pull the screw into place, but a drill is also a type of screw. In this case the drill bit is fixed so that the thread pulls material outward in order to create a hole.

As the auger is turned clockwise by a motor on the crane, the thread pulls it into the ground.

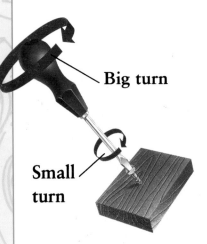

Big turn

Small turn

A screwdriver works like a lever. A smaller force used to make a big turn in the screwdriver becomes a bigger force used to make a small turn in the screw, pushing it hard into the wood.

Ramps and screws

1 You can think of a screw as a ramp wrapped around a pole. To see this yourself, take a pencil and wrap a triangular piece of paper (the ramp) around it (*below*).

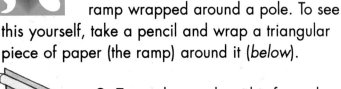

2 To see how a thread is formed, take two pieces of string, and wind them around the pencil, side by side. Now if you remove one of the pieces of string you will be left with a thread on the pencil.

Once the auger is buried in the ground, the crane can use its compound pulley to lift it, and the earth trapped in its threads, upward.

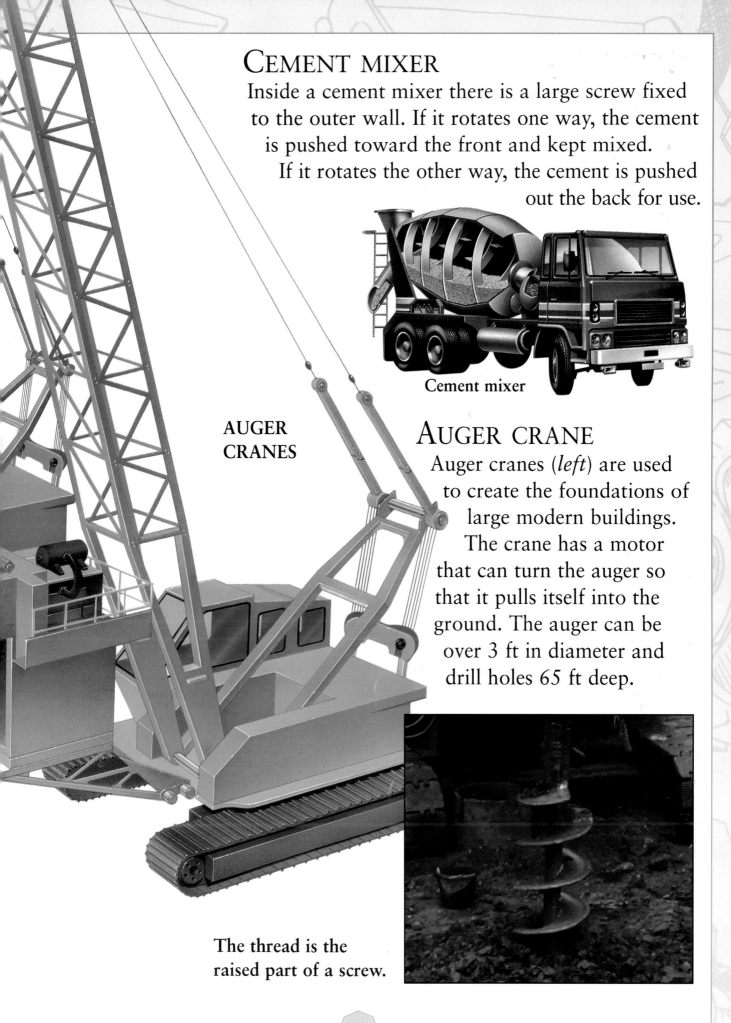

CEMENT MIXER

Inside a cement mixer there is a large screw fixed to the outer wall. If it rotates one way, the cement is pushed toward the front and kept mixed.
If it rotates the other way, the cement is pushed out the back for use.

Cement mixer

AUGER CRANES

AUGER CRANE

Auger cranes (*left*) are used to create the foundations of large modern buildings. The crane has a motor that can turn the auger so that it pulls itself into the ground. The auger can be over 3 ft in diameter and drill holes 65 ft deep.

The thread is the raised part of a screw.

CHAPTER 3 – POWER

Building machines and tractors don't move very fast. But they move and lift enormous loads—a big truck can pull up to 600 tons—so they need a very powerful engine.

Nowadays, this is usually a diesel engine and it is often used to provide the power for the hydraulic system (see page 20).

WHAT IS POWER?

Power is the rate of doing work. A task requires the same amount of work whether done quickly or slowly. But greater power is needed to do the work quickly.

For example, a person can supply the energy to move a car (*below*). However, the car will only move slowly, as a person is not very powerful. An engine can supply the same amount of energy in a shorter time.

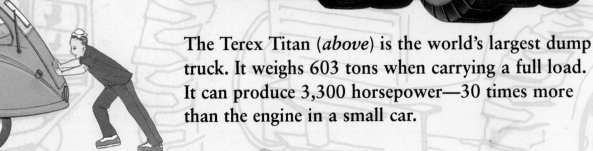

The Terex Titan (*above*) is the world's largest dump truck. It weighs 603 tons when carrying a full load. It can produce 3,300 horsepower—30 times more than the engine in a small car.

1 **SLING YOUR HOOK**
Thread string from the winch over the dowel on the crane arm and through the eyelet attached to the bead. Then tie the end to the eyelet that is fixed to the crane arm.

Winch

Diesel fuel is cheaper to use than gasoline—especially important in fuel-guzzling monsters like the one above. Big trucks also have up to 20 forward and 4 reverse gears to make the most efficient use of the engine.

HYDRAULIC TRAIN

Sometimes it is more efficient to have only one source of power for all of the motors in a complex machine. Hydraulic trains use a single engine to provide the power to pump a liquid at high pressure to motors attached to each wheel.

ELECTRIC POWER

Tower cranes (*right*) are often powered by electric motors because it's much easier to carry electricity to the top of the crane in wires than to carry diesel in pipes that might leak.

HYDRAULICS

Hydraulic systems are another way of changing the direction and size of a force. An engine is used to pump a liquid at high pressure down narrow pipes. The liquid pushes against a piston inside a cylinder, forcing it to move.

Try this experiment!

Hydraulic project

1 Find a thick plastic bag with no holes in it, such as a freezer bag. Seal the end with sticky tape and insert a piece of plastic pipe.

2 Lay the bag on the floor and place a solid board on top. Then fill the pipe with water from a jug and connect it to the end of a plastic bottle full of water. All the joints need to be well sealed.

3 Now stand on the board and squeeze the plastic bottle. You will feel yourself being pushed up by the water in the bag!

Piston rod

Piston rod moves up

1 Liquid pumped into the piston through narrow pipes pushes the piston rod out with a very large force.

2 Another piston is used to rotate the scoop to pick up soil.

20

MODEL CRANE
PART 5

THE BUCKET ARM

1 MAKE THE ARM

Cut out two part **N**s and parts **P** and **O** from thick cardboard. Glue supports (**P** and **O**) to the two part **N**s. Next, cut a 1 in length of dowel and screw an eyelet into the dowel. Then glue this dowel to the top of the arms.

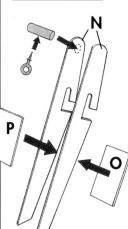

Arm

R

S

Bucket

2 MAKING THE BUCKET

Cut out two part **Q**s and part **R** from thick cardboard, and part **S** from thin cardboard. Glue the two **Q**s to the edges of part **S**. Once the glue has dried, glue part **R** to the top edge of **S** and **Q**.

R

Q

Q

S

3 ATTACH BUCKET TO ARM

Once the glue on the bucket and the arm are dry, glue the base of the arm to the center of **R** and the top of **S**.

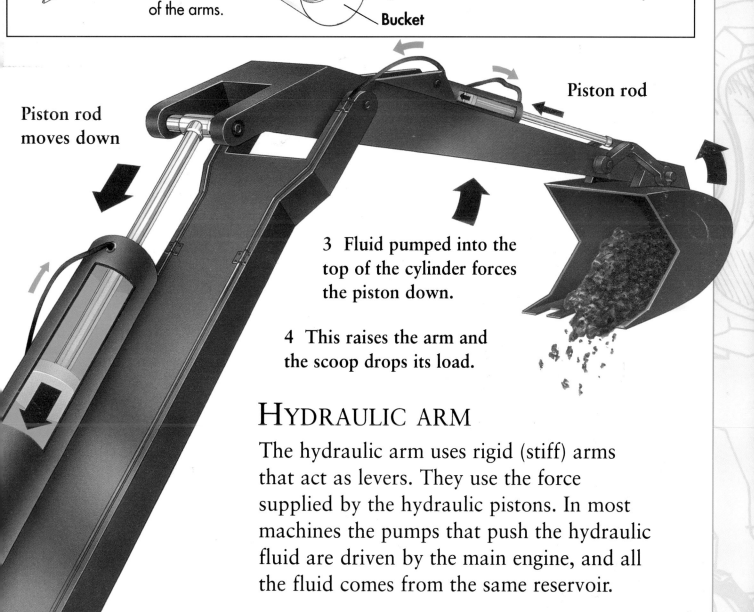

Piston rod moves down

Piston rod

3 Fluid pumped into the top of the cylinder forces the piston down.

4 This raises the arm and the scoop drops its load.

HYDRAULIC ARM

The hydraulic arm uses rigid (stiff) arms that act as levers. They use the force supplied by the hydraulic pistons. In most machines the pumps that push the hydraulic fluid are driven by the main engine, and all the fluid comes from the same reservoir.

Pneumatic project

Gases squashed against solid objects can force them to move. Make a gas by adding bakingsoda to vinegar in a plastic bottle. Pour in half a cup of vinegar, then wrap the soda in a twist of paper and add it to the bottle. Push a cork into the bottle and the pressure of the gas will force it out.

BACKHOE DRILLER

The hydraulic motor of the digger pumps fluid into and out of the piston of the drill in short, sharp bursts.

At the same time the pistons of the arm press down on the drill to force it into the ground.

CHAPTER 4 – CONTROLS

Pneumatics (systems that use compressed air) and hydraulics (systems that use compressed liquids) are both used to control building machines.

Pneumatics are less efficient because the air heats up as it is squashed, but they are simpler because air is simply sucked in from outside.

You can create the pressure to pop a cork without using chemicals. If you squeeze a bottle by jumping on it, it has the same effect. Be careful!

MODEL CRANE
PART 6

BUCKET ARM

Bucket arm

1 ADD BUCKET ARM
Hook the arm onto the dowel cross bar at the top of the crane arm. Then tie the string from the winch to the eyelet which is connected to the bead and hook.

2 OPERATE BUCKET ARM
Connect the hook on the string to the eyelet on the bucket arm's cross bar. Now you are ready to operate the bucket arm— just turn the winch handle and lift the bucket.

Winch handle

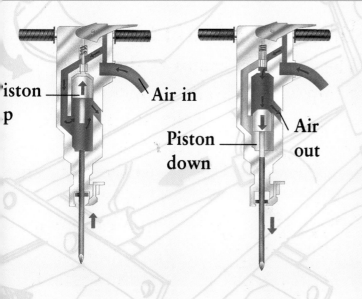

Piston
up

Air in

Piston
down

Air
out

PNEUMATIC DRILL

Pneumatic drills use compressed air instead of a fluid to power the drill. Air is pumped from a compressor into the drill. A heavy weight inside the drill is pushed up or down by a series of valves that control the flow of air. The air is then released into the outside world which is why this kind of drill is so noisy.

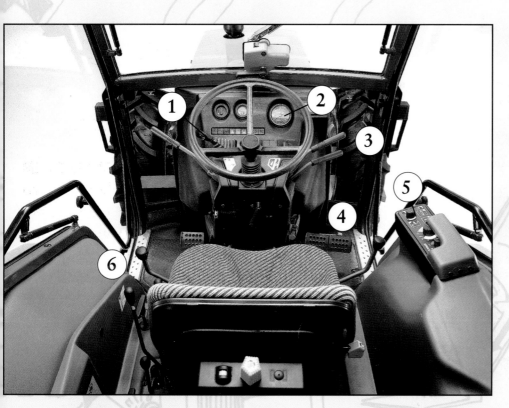

INSIDE THE CAB

1. Lever to select forward or reverse
2. Instrument panel
3. Levers for horn, road and indicator lights
4. Brake and accelerator pedals
5. Starter switch and heating controls
6. Hydraulic control levers

THE CAB

The cab of any vehicle provides protection for the driver and controls to operate the machine. Many controls operate the valves of the hydraulic system. Though there are many systems, the digger only needs one engine.

Power steering (*right*) uses hydraulics to push the wheels to the side. The fluid pumped into the cylinders moves the pistons in and out.

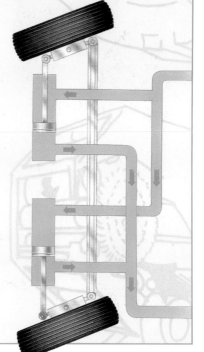

TRUCK SYSTEMS

Trucks carry loads from one place to another. But they still have to do lifting. Every time they travel uphill they lift themselves and their load. The wheels change the turning force of the engine into a force that drives the truck forward. Trucks also use hydraulic systems for dumping their load and for steering.

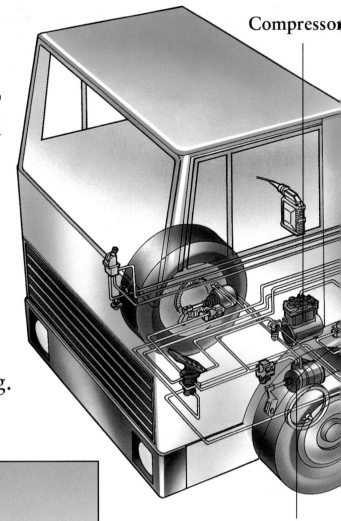

Compressor

Brake unit on each wheel

Ram stretches upward.

Fluid is pumped in through pipes.

Gluing on the track section

Road trucks have a smooth shape to reduce drag.

HYDRAULIC RAMS

Trucks use hydraulic rams to dump their load. A ram works like the pistons in a hydraulic arm, but it stretches like a telescope to many times its length. Several tubes inside each other can be pushed out by hydraulic fluid.

Air is forced between the rim of the wheels and the brake pads. When the air is released, the pads clamp against the wheels.

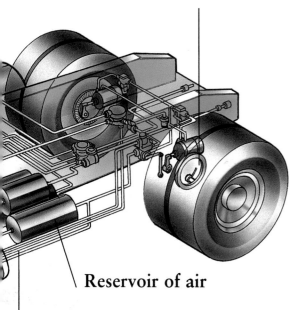

Reservoir of air

Brake lines connect the compressor to the brake units.

AIR BRAKES

Most trucks have air brakes. These use high-pressure air supplied by a compressor. The air pushes in between the inner rim of the wheel and the brake pads or shoes.

When the driver puts his or her foot on the brake, the air is released and the pads spring against the wheels, stopping the truck.

A fork lift truck carries standard loads. Its forks fit underneath a palette or container. Then it uses hydraulic rams to lift and stack the load.

TRUCK CABS

Truck drivers spend long hours on the road, so their cabs are built for comfort.

1 Citizen's Broadcast (CB) radio
2 Instrument panel
3 Folding tables for maps
4 Plenty of storage space
5 Bed

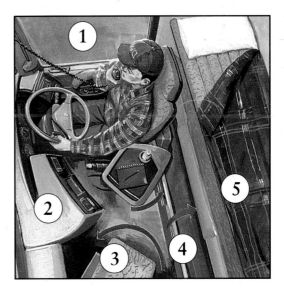

MODEL CRANE
PART 7
ADD THE PIVOT

1 MAKE THE LOWER PIVOT Cut part **T** out of thick cardboard and gently roll it over a large cardboard tube. Glue its ends together.

T

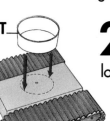

2 ADD PIVOT TO WHEEL BASE When the glue is dry on the lower pivot, glue **T** onto the dotted circle on the wheel base.

ALL-PURPOSE TRACTORS

Testing the finished model

The word tractor means "a machine for pulling and pushing." But by connecting different attachments to the front and back, a tractor performs an enormous range of tasks. The heavy engine and hydraulic systems are low down to make the tractor stable, and a strong cab protects the driver if the tractor does roll.

Strong cab

Large wheels for extra grip

HEAVY LIFTING

The hydraulic system of the tractor can power an arm with a boom, dipper, and bucket. For very heavy loads a counterweight can be attached at the back.

MODEL CRANE
PART 8

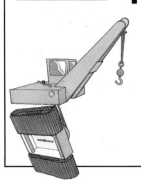

THE FINISHED CRANE

1 TO FINISH YOUR CRANE
Paint all parts of the crane. Then feed a rubber band through the holes in the middle of **F** and **T**. Finally, put a matchstick through the loops at each end to hold **F** and **T** together.

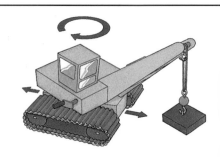

2 WORK THE MODEL
Your model is now complete. You can use it as a crane or add the digger attachment with the bucket.

PULLING

Tractors that are used for plowing the soil need to be able to pull with enormous force. The large back wheels provide good grip and spread the load on soft ground.

Powerful engine

Hydraulic systems for attachments front and back

BACKHOE DIGGING

When used with a digging or lifting arm at the back (*below*), hydraulic legs help prevent the tractor tipping as the load is moved to the side.

BACKHOE DRILL

A shovel can be used as a lever to apply force. By holding the shovel down at the front, the force on the drill increases because the shovel acts as the fulcrum of a lever (*left*).

FORCE and WORK

A force is the scientific name for a push or a pull. If a force moves something this gives energy to the object. Work is another name for energy. When somebody or something does a lot of work, they are transferring a lot of energy from one object to another.

SIMPLE MACHINES

In the ancient world there were five simple machines: the wheel, the lever, the pulley, the screw, and the ramp. Each of these could be used by a person to lift weights that were too heavy to be lifted on their own.

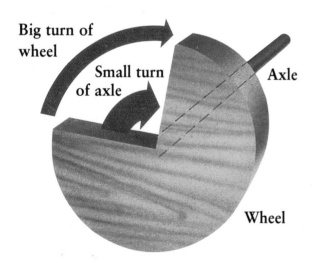

Big turn of wheel

Small turn of axle

Axle

Wheel

WHEELS and AXLES

Axles work like levers (*above*). When the axle makes a small turn with a big force, the wheel turns a larger distance with a smaller force. The axle is smaller, so there is less friction where it joins the vehicle.

LEVERS

A lever allows a small force moving a long way to create a big force that moves a short distance. The simplest lever is a rigid bar that twists about a point called the fulcrum. This is a first-class lever (e.g. scales), with the fulcrum between the load and the effort.

A second-class lever (e.g. bottle opener) has the load between the fulcrum and the effort. In a third-class lever (e.g. tweezers), the effort is between the fulcrum and the load.

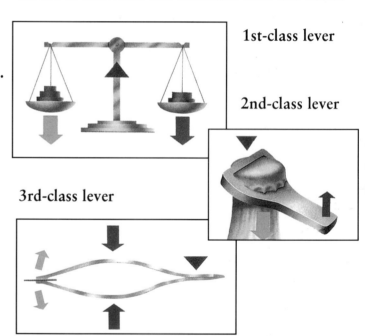

1st-class lever

2nd-class lever

3rd-class lever

? *1 Can you remember what class of levers a wheelbarrow and a seesaw are? Answers to all questions on pages 28–29 are on page 32.*

PULLEYS

A pulley allows a person to lift something up while staying put on the ground. Several pulleys joined together make a compound pulley (*right*). On a compound pulley, pulling the rope a long way raises a heavy weight a short distance.

? 2a *Why do some vehicles have caterpillar tracks?* 2b *Where should their weight be to make them stable?*

SCREWS

A screw works like a lever. A smaller force that makes a big turn in the top of the screw becomes a bigger force used to make a small turn in the screw, pushing it hard into the wood.

RAMPS

A ramp helps a person to increase the distance over which he or she moves an object against the force of gravity. The longer the ramp, the less force is needed to lift the load.

? 3 *Can you remember the good and bad points about using pneumatic rather than hydraulic systems?*

TECHNICAL TERMS

Balanced – a vehicle or object that does not fall over on its own.

Compound – a system with more than one part, e.g. a compound lever combines two or more levers.

Compressor – a machine that squashes air into a smaller space, creating the high-pressure air that is used in pneumatic systems.

Hydraulic arm

Counterweight – the weight used to balance the load on a crane or truck.

Drag – when air flows past an object and slows it down.

Fulcrum – the pivot of a lever.

Gravity – the force that pulls everything around us down toward the ground. Gravity also pulls any two objects toward each other.

Hydraulic – a machine that uses oil pumped at high pressure to push against a piston.

Jib – the long arm on a crane.

Pneumatic – a machine that works using compressed (squashed) air.

Stable – a vehicle that falls back to its original position if it leans over.

Thread – the raised part of a screw that grips the wood or ground it is being drilled into.

Traction – the scientific word for grip.

VEHICLE PARTS

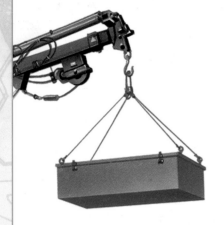

Trucks and tractors look quite different but have many similar systems, such as diesel engines and hydraulic pumps. Most cranes are fixed to the ground so they do not need braking or steering systems. They are driven by electric motors.

1 STEERING WHEEL
Tractors and trucks have hydraulic power steering.

2 ENGINE
Many tractors and most trucks have diesel engines. In diesel engines the fuel is set alight by air that has been heated up to 4,500°F by compression.

3 FOUR-WHEEL DRIVE
Big tractors have four-wheel drive for extra grip.

4 TIRES
Off-road vehicles have tires with a large tread for added traction.

5 HYDRAULICS
The hydraulic system controls the working position of attachments hitched to or mounted on the tractor.

6 PTO
The power take-off (PTO) provides power for machines pulled by the tractor, such as spray pumps and potato diggers.

WHEELS QUIZ
A-D show some different truck and tractor wheels. Can you spot which vehicle they come from? Answers on page 32.

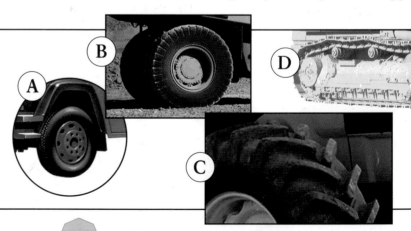

TRACTOR

The tractor is also the name for the front part of a truck and includes the engine and cab. A cab provides a safe place for a driver to work in.

8 GEARS

Large trucks have up to 20 forward and 4 reverse gears to make the most efficient use of their engine in all weathers.

ATTACHMENTS

Trucks, tractors, and cranes use a variety of hydraulic and pneumatic systems.

Can you recognize what these lifting and digging systems are? The answers are on page 32.

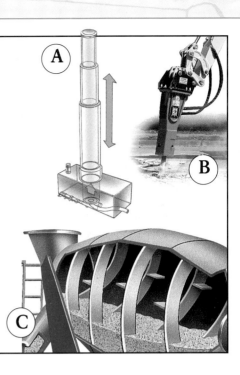

11 TANK

Tanks are used to carry compressed gas or liquids such as milk.

13 ELECTRIC MOTOR

Cranes are driven by electric motors to avoid the danger of fire from a leaking fuel pipe.

14 JIB

A crane's main arm.

15 PULLEYS

Compound pulleys are used to lift heavy loads.

16 BUCKETS

Buckets are used to lift wet concrete.

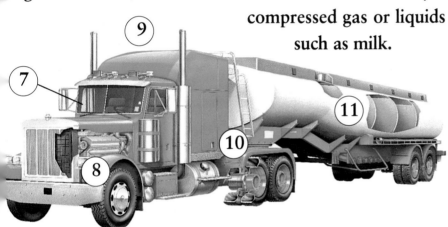

9 STREAMLINING

Drag slows down any moving object as it travels. Many trucks have a long, smooth shape to reduce drag.

12 COUNTERWEIGHTS

Heavy weights, often big blocks of concrete, are used to balance the load lifted by a crane.

10 TRAILER

The load is carried in a trailer that is hitched to the tractor.

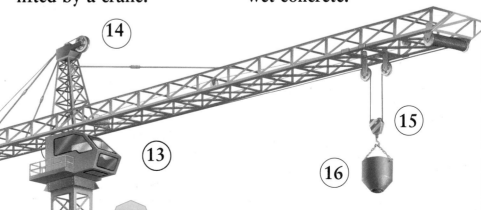

INDEX

The finished model crane

Answers: Pages 28–29
1 A wheelbarrow is a second-class lever and a seesaw is a first-class lever. **2a** Tracks spread the weight of a vehicle on soft ground. They also provide good grip and keep the vehicle stable.

2b The weight (the engine and the load) should be kept as close to the ground as possible. **3** The air in a pneumatic system heats up when it is compressed and this wastes energy. But unlike the liquid in hydraulic systems, air can be pumped in from the outside so it doesn't need to be recycled. **Page 30 A** = mobile crane, p.15, **B** = monster truck, p.19, **C** = tractor, p.5, **D** = bulldozer, p.6. **Page 31 A** = hydraulic ram in a truck, p.24, **B** = backhoe drill, p. 27, **C** = concrete mixer, p.17.

PHOTO CREDITS
Abbreviations—t – top, m– middle, b – bottom, r – right, l – left, c – center:
1, 8-9—Scania. 2, 12—JCB. 4-5, 6—CAT. 5bl, 23, 26, 27l, 27tr, 30br—Renault. 7—Frank Spooner Pictures. 5tr, 8bl—Liebherr. 8c, 27mr, 27bl, 30mr—John Deere. 11, 17, 19br—Select Pictures. 14t—Sunderland Shipbuilders. 19tl, 30mb—Digital Stock. 22—Paul Nightingale. 24—Solution Pictures.